Thoughts of a mentally ill

I have written my thoughts to offer them to all, just or wrong these are, I hope that you like and bring you to a greater knowledge about the shortcomings, defects and virtues of what are the true mentally ill, as well as reflections of the case.

In this review I entered in the queue, some of my imaginary tales.

Rev. 3   *Antonio Piantini*

Summary

To my doctor

Dear Doctor, I am Antonio Piantini and I wanted to ask you a pleasure: I would like to write a book about my thoughts or poems in short everything that goes through my head, to make it known to others too.

I wanted to ask you if it was possible to involve all mentally ill those who want to let everyone know, a thought, a phrase, a poem, signed with their own name, to let the world know that we exist and we can say our thoughts even if under voice, because for the society we count nothing, or we are even just a burden for others, including family members.

I would be very grateful doctor if you wanted to consider this my proposal, and I wait for an answer.

If in writing this book selling there will be a profit, I leave to you the free decision of how to share the money earned.

Distinct Greetings from *Antonio Piantini*.

The forest

More I think life is long, more I realize it is short for all the ideas I want to achieve, all over time it lengthens. I thought to do in my land this park in a short time one or two years instead they have spent so many that or even lost the account of past years.

I would like in life to do something as big as this park of giant sequoias to be remembered that even a small person but with great ideas, with little cost of seed and loam, can create with the help of public institutions, something as giant as can be the

Colosseum or the pyramids or other millenary buildings, but this idea of mine is even more beautiful because to realize it, do not want slaves nor whips to beat the people but people who love the woods, who love plants, and like to live in a planet where nature does its part.

I would like this park of mine was not simply a forest of redwoods, all together as a forestry but that was as expanded as possible, in order to give the impression of a natural forest and with the game of the plants that are already there when the sequoias will exceed them in height of several meters, the visual impact should be beautiful.

I when I say forest have confusion in my mind because, what is the real forest, that we are accustomed to see where is grouped a single species for example a forest of just chestnuts near a small wood of pines, where it's nice to go looking for mushrooms, or a forest of young oak or even fir or beech trees, or the real forest is that of the forest of the Lama, where there are many varieties of tree, bushes and herbs.

In the wood of Lama I saw Lime -trees, Ashes, Maples, Alders, Hornbeam, Pines and especially I saw so many people who loved that kind of forest where you can still to see the fruit of the plant of the beautiful woman, who used women to magnify the pupils to make themselves so more attractive. Where you see the heaps of fir needles made from the ants, high even more than one meter.

I think that the variety of trees creates even more robust and less susceptible individuals because each tree subtracts from the soil different substances from species to species and the organic material created by the decomposition of the leaves of multiple types of trees is definitely better than the leaves of a tree species only. I'll never get tired of saying one thing: The more the woods and the more diverse the more beautiful, and how the romans put the chestnut trees to feed the mountain populations, and until recently used again to feed, I think that the chestnut is now declining and can be accompanied with other and essences of trees type Ash, Maples lindens etc. I think if in Casentino you want tourism, you have to largely recreate a forest like that of the Lama.

Help others

But!: What I do in the world I do not know, giving a reason to its existence is a difficult thing, I have tried to give you a reason by giving birth to trees in the way of extinction and then give them to everyone hoping that some tree can live.

I did family with a beautiful and talented wife, who married me while knowing about my illness (depressive maniac), and she loves me as much as I want. I have two beautiful girls who sometimes quarrel but then make peace right away. I have a beautiful house, two quarters that I will leave to my two daughters. But the reason for each of us to live a life with a sense that escapes out of the mass is to help for what is possible who needs help whether they are people or not, help without ask for anything in return, for the mere reason of having joy in the give help to those who has need.

I try to help the trees in the way of extinction, but I appreciate much more who helps people like the elderly handicapped physical or psychic children with any handicap, while making it free without to have in return no money. This is the real sense of giving the life of each of us, without being heroes or Saints, but to give, to give and to give love to all.

Planet Earth

To love this planet,

Why to love this planet,

What to love about this planet

The Earth the only planet that knows the man in whom he can live, a planet full of life that man wants to recreate at his leisure and interest favoring animal and plant species useful and pleasing to him, undoing every human plant animal living or fish that do not create an immediate economic gain, not calculating in the future of hundreds of years.

This planet is wonderful for its variety of peoples and human races, which will miss within a few tens of years, because the poorest peoples are attracted by the wealthiest nations of technology as if they were wealthy countries, and when they flee from their villages to come to the countries so rich people realize they are not well accepted rejected by society and enclosed all together, often, if they find work, they are poorly paid jobs or jobs that don't want to be wealthy.

When even one man goes away from his own village, from his own land where he was born and where has learned to survive by knowing all the nature that surrounds it, trees of the forest that feed it for free, which with their chemicals cure it from serious or less serious diseases, and with wild animals and fish always available for feed, when one man goes away, one loses a source of immense knowledge that the technological man often does not appreciate, even when he arrives with his own means scrapers chainsaws and matches destroys everything creating pastures for his own beasts.

What world is better I do not know, if that technological where everyone runs in search of what we do not have for to buy it, or the world of those who do not know the technology and that It lives as being superior among the animals and the forest.

Life changing

In 1901 who had the land to be cultivated, as an example a farm, with beasts that could working the earth, with animals that gave milk, cheeses, meat and if in more they had the luck of having a chestnut forest that gave them with chestnuts, a eat at low cost, they were considered as people who were fine. If people then had more of a farm and they needed a factor to manage them and profit plots, they were the real gentlemen, the way people live in time changes, fascinated by the cities where life is more comfortable and work are more profitable and the new industries that grow like mushrooms where work is less tiring than in campaigns and the pay is good that allows you to keep the whole family, if the family works in two can even buy house, so many young people go away from countryside to go to the city. Explodes the bum construction, palaces are built always more high, thanks to the reinforced concrete, to meet market needs so many farms, the least profitable, and also other were abandoned or remain to cultivate them, for that they can do, older people, many houses colonies once abandoned in a few years begin to ruin and to fall, *a big loss for the landscape of Italian campaigns*.

In 2001 the life of man changes, the work in the factories is not more well paid, to camp family today you need working in two if that's enough, competition from countries of eastern Europe and China in addition to the countries of the South East Asian, they put in crisis not to say on their knees our companies and people last hard to find work.

Construction does not pull more the market because there are too many apartments for sale, the only thing is the makeover of farmhouses that had once been abandoned.

THE FUTURE WHAT WILL BE? Each person has their own point of view, 100 people 100 different thoughts, it is not easy to find all of the usual opinion. I say my right or wrong that it is:

THE FUTURE in my opinion will be of the common ones that make more their urban areas and campaigns, helping the integration of people who come from other peoples, from other continents and so on, because the diversity of races, species animals and plants and more, it is the true richness of a nation, region and municipality. The industrial era will be a big resizing causes the competition of the developing countries development, and not can be infinitely the driving wheel.

The environment in the coming years according me will be the wheel of the tow truck.

Building parks in own suburbs with variety of trees all over the world (allowing the climate and land permit) to make avenues of trees or plant grove, recover forests now abandoned or cultivated with two or three species of trees, commonly cut, and convert them to high trunk with more variety of species although not autochthonous, to become beautiful and fascinating landscape.

I live in the countryside around me there are so many woods though me are not so beautiful because: first of all, many are cut periodically to make wood from burn, so there are no big plants, according to other high-stem forests consist of a single species of tree making the landscape and how sad, because free of contrasting colors and size scaling.

THE FUTURE for me does not have to be the tourist who is from another country with a swollen wallet of money, ready to be plucked, or so poor as to be exploited and treated as a slave and humiliated all the days, I think the future is when ordinary people feel tourist also in own cities, in the municipalities in the environment where live every days, feel fascinated by the beauty of architectures of the man and the wonderful and extravagant beauty of the trees of variety endless and bushes with infinite flowers, the future is not of who has money and not even those who has many bricks, the future in my opinion is who sows in the environment, convinced that very soon will pick up his fruits.

Psychosis

Life that funny thing, but if you say no one laughs, has said Francesco Guccini in one of his songs.

Life for a mentally ill is just funny, adjust with the chemistry ingested by mouth its own thoughts its sadness or euphoria, irritability or quiet, want to work or do nothing, adjust your own sleep more or less hours, no longer be masters of one's life if you don't have to sing a bag of drugs, if my life was like that of an electric motor that once disconnected the plug stops without any pain, rip the thorn of my life, because if a person does not pass us in a mental illness cannot understand the pain that it proves.

To make a summary of my illness I will start from the beginning in 1993 from August to October, when I came the acute psychosis in three forms of delirium, before addict after it became a homosexual, and the last delirium perhaps the worst, the mystical delirium , terrifying it seems to live to make the idea inside the movie The Exorcist, with the difference that in the film you can disconnect the plug or change channel in my reality I lived there 24 hours a day, I was terrified in my head I felt the voice of God that as a friend had become a commanding voice, and he always got angry with me because he said I was bad, the other auditory and visual hallucinations were of the devil, more than anything annoyed me the snoring of my mother who for me was the head of the Devils and since I slept little, 3 hours per night, this snoring kept me awake and still terrified motionless until the morning. The day I heard the devil speak with the voice of my relatives and friends, to my sister and one of our clients I saw the tongue outside the mouth like that of a snake, every puff or rustling that you can look like the blowing of the serpent makes you believe that be the devil etc. etc. in October I took the medicine (although for me with those medicines they wanted me to poison) Serenase the night I made a sleep from king, after months I slept A few hours. Thereafter I always taken the medicine, but the mood swings during the year or week in week they'll destroy you, you can't say you I'll be working all week because it's enough that a little thing is going to be crooked and the whole world falls off.

Antonio Piantini

I love life

I love life, although I attempted suicide three times by ingesting handfuls of psychotropic drugs.

I love life, especially the life of the weakest beings who cannot even move like the trees that stand still and wait for their fate, to be burned or sawn by the man Without Pity.

And with them when they burn thousands of insects of reptiles and even animals that do not make it to escape, to get away from this disaster that is often caused from man, without reflecting the damage it does.

Trees, these living beings that give so much to life on this planet, offer oxygen and wood to cook and heat the man, how can you remove them burning life when they are standing still alive. I don't know but to give fire to a forest you have to hate this planet and the life that's in it, I don't know but maybe who gives fire are sick minds who do not love anyone's life, and think that this planet offers life to more extravagant and absurd beings, such as the whale and the gnat, or the violet and the sequoia. Absurd thing but so beautiful and fascinating the diversity of the living beings of the Earth, a treasure that man must preserve.

Autumn

Each person has a season of the year that he likes more, there are those who like the most winter because you go to the mountains to ski on the snow, there are those who like the spring for the awakening of nature with flowers and scents of plants, there are those who like the most summer because it's hot and you can go to the sea to swim, for everyone there is a season that likes more than the other, to me most of all I like the Autumn because nature is illuminated by a thousand colors and almost all vivid from yellow to red and then brown, I like it because you go to look for mushrooms and when we are in the woods you feel raining the leaves on the ground with a sweet rustle, like the chestnuts that when fall tumble on the ground and when it rains and falls the fog the forest assumes a spooky face that makes you rejoice when from the fog you appear the vision of a deer with long branched horns and his mighty stature, which before realizing it was evaporated in the fog. The autumn month in which it is more willing to eat and drink a good glass of wine the chestnuts roasted with the frying pan on the fiery and flaming fire and a night spent in the company to say balderdash for then go in bed a little drunk for drinking a glass of wine too. Past times and memories of when the vigils were made in two three families in front of the roaring fire for the burnt chestnut. Today the time has changed, with the arrival of the television families have lost that way of getting together to party every night as he used to, now all locked in the house with a thousand padlocks for the fear of thieves we ruin our lives, and we lose very often respect and trust in others.

Good or bad

Many times we wonder if there is something outside of us, like a spirit apart from good that him can give us light in our thoughts. In truth, this spirit exists, but instead of being outside of us lies within us in our hearts in our minds, and with him we speak by seeking a little comfort to our every problem, yes because in our brain everything is divided into good or evil and depends on us what we want to give more space both in our behavior and in our thoughts, certainly we cannot always choose one thing of the two, would not human, but we must try especially in choosing the part of the good.

In sick minds this good or evil increases in value, and often makes us to think that inside us is the devil or God and everything is complicated to make the right choice of our behavior, because if we unfortunately choose evil it happens that in our delirium to be able to hurt to someone even to our relatives.

The factors that in our brain damage these behaviors of good or bad are two chemicals, dopamine and serotonin, the first is the substance of the soul of each of us and the second is the Substance that controls the mood depression or euphoria.

Today there are many medicines to treat the mentally ill, but often they are refused by the sick, because not the year the concept of being sick.

Happy Birthday Maria

Dear Maria in this letter I wanted to wish you happy birthday for the fifty years that you fulfill and I wish you to accomplish more in my company, because I am very much in love with you and I would like to stay as long as possible with you. These past years together I hope they have been the best in life spent, and I hope that the years that will come in the future are even better.

I love you so much, Mary I'm just so fond of you and I would do anything you asked me to stay with you. These past years together are the most beautiful in my life, where I realized as a person by putting a family on my feet thanks to your great help.

We have a nice house that you keep very clean kept and we have furnished together with what we liked most.

I wish you so much happiness in the future, and to be able to stay healthy, this and what matters most, I know that these words of mine will not be the best that one can write, because I am not a writer, but I am only a lover, in love with you Maria.

Antonio Piantini

Countryside and City

The city where man lives from a sense of a large hive where man lives eats and works, but on Sunday all outside the city to live a different day in the countryside or in the mountains or the sea, to relax from the bustle of the city and the fatigue of work. The city where the night all lights up to a thousand colors and in the evening invites people to leave the house, who for a walk to see shops, who to meet their friends and stop at a few bars to have a chat and then go to the cinema or some nightclub.

And the campaign? In the campaign in the evening they remain open a few bars, youth hangout or for older people to do some card game while in the summer lights no even countries outside the city, organizing festivals parties or fairs.

The campaign that for the eye of those who pass careless or fast does not say anything, for those who are full of colors, not enlightened like those of cities, but perhaps more real and more beautiful for those who live there, and every season gives its fruits and its colors, the big and old trees in countryside are like monuments of a big city and the woods are like so many houses of a city.

It is nice to walk through the paths of the forest and recognize where it takes you, just like the road of a city, recognizing the trees, as you recognize the neighborhoods of the city, recognize the mushrooms, as you recognize the shops of the city, in short! The countryside has a pinch of city.

Dear Mr. Vincenzo

Dear Mr. Vincenzo, I'm sorry to disturb you again, But, I came to mind where to put the giant sequoias I made to be born. I would like to make an avenue that for example starts from above to Cetica and arrives up in Pratomagno, or from the road that comes from Poppi to the border with Castel San Niccolò beginning to plant them up from Pratomagno. I of plants I have a little, more than 500, and put at the distance of 10 m., steering the road, right and left, you get to cover a length of 5km.

Make an avenue so surely between 100 years will be a wonderful thing to pass with the car in the midst of these beasts of 2,5m/3m in diameter, and feeling small in front to such a wonder of nature.

Giant Sequoias are not trees equal to the others, but they are the largest living beings on the planet Earth, and they are also endangered since in America they have stood as many as the surface of the municipalities of Castel San Niccolò, Montemignaio and Ortignano-Raggiolo. What is for sure is that it will leave to future generations something that lasts millennia, since the Sequoias live up to 3,500 years being among the longest-lived plants of the earth.

Thank you for your interest in the problem.   Distinct Greetings
Antonio Piantini

Who we are, we and the others

Who we are, and what we think others are.

In my opinion we see in the others our defects or merits, for example: If we are jealous we believe that the others envy us, if we are bad and spiteful we think that others are so with us that is bad and spiteful, if we are racist so we think that others are with us, if we tease people by habit so we believe that the others behave so with us, if we steal so we think that others want stealing things to us, if we have a good character so we think that other people have our own character, if we are honest and do not steal so we believe that others are with us, in sum we see other people not really for what they are, but we identify them for that is our flaw of character, good or bad that we are.

Noticing their own flaws and difficult, and correcting them and even more difficult.

In judging the other good or bad you should do an examination of conscience and understand who we actually are and what we believe others think of us without being hypocritical but honest with themselves.

What make you good or bad

I do not know how to describe it but for a mentally ill every day is not equal to the previous, just little to make you feel good or bad. Just a day of good weather and It pulls you a little more in mood, if it is a cloudy day and it rains or is cold, you feel sadder and anxious e so the mood also changes with changing seasons, with euphoric summers and autumn and more melancholy and depressed winters.

But being cheerful or sad also changes with what we eat, for example if we eat a little chocolate pulls us an up, but what changes more behavior is mainly the ingestion of chemicals present in psychotropic drugs, which can make you good and quiet or agitated and anguished internally without manifested outwardly.

However, psychotropic drugs should also be changed from one season to the other or even from one day to the other, in short having a psychic disorder creates a big problem for be well, and often it is not well understood by the family because they see you feel good one day and another no. Certain psychotropic drugs work and they make you feel good others make you feel bad, and not to all people work in equal firmly, also the behavior of other people in your comparisons can make you feel bad or not, in short it is well not so easy.

Dedicated to You

This thought I want to dedicate it to the last ones, those who never win a medal, those who have flies in the face and no longer have the strength to remove away from the face, those who are born and shortly after dying of hunger.

I dedicate this thought even to those bums who eat go to rummage in the dumpsters, and to sleep they go under the bridges, and as sheets use the cartoons and newspapers, they are remembered only for Christmas parties or when it is very cold because some die frozen.

I dedicate my thoughts to those who are born with any disease, and have to face the world uphill without any pity.

I dedicate my thoughts to all those who do not have never received an education, never been to school, and are swindled by people who school have made too much and they know the laws well and how to make them turn to their own gain.

I dedicate my thoughts to all those who suffer both physical and psychic violence, and not year the strength to defend themselves and are forced every day to feel humiliated and oppressed.

I dedicate this my thoughts to all those who humbly go to work every day just to have the fortune to span if and the own family.

Depression

It's a year that I have alternate depression with moments that I'm fine for three four days then I return the major depression where you do nothing but think how to die.

In the past years or attempted suicide twice by ingesting many psychotropic drugs, and they saved by making me twice the gastric lavage.

It's terrible depression and it's not understood by who does not never had, footsteps of days to weep because it is so strong psychic pain that you can't do anything. Many think that mentally ill are vagabonds because many times they are at home without doing anything, those people are mistaken because the pain of a mental illness is such that it exceeds many other diseases with physical handicaps. The mentally ill are only the most sensitive people in the world around them, they are sick for a word that is dictated by the voice a little higher or when one looks at you with a way how angry he was for your presence, however for those who have a mental ill at home the only help he can give him is to check that he takes the medicines that prescribed the psychiatrist, because often the mentally ill have consciousness of one's illness and so many times they refuse it.

Ecology

I am just a passenger on this land spaceship, a passenger as one of the millions of men who inhabit this world, one that does not count anything and no voice in anything because I'm crazy, discarded by the society of the healthy.

The world I dream of is a world in which who commands the

government has another aspiration instead make money or reign as a dictator, but love their own people, love their own land and to protect from who makes a bad use of it, polluting it with residues of all types.

The land in which we live is the only place in the universe where man can live, and people must understand that there are hundreds or thousands of living animals and plants in the critical area of extinction, after which there are no more, disappeared from the earth.

For this a good government should recreate the appropriate environment to try to save more species from the extinction, because it will come a day that we'll notice that we have made a splurge, run all those behind the money printed paper and not open the eyes to see that we are destroying our house. People: whose majority lives in cities similar to large beehives, which he doesn't care if he disappears from the world a plant to which insects and animals are connected, or an ecosystem has collapsed to make way for a forestry, that is, only one species of tree, beech, fir, pinewood, chestnut, woods of only oaks, it is so destroyed all an ecosystem just because a man comes back more comfortable having only one essence all together because so grouped is done first to work it and to gain in less time more money, and so they disappeared from our woods plants that today not even the imagination to think that there were been, such as: the major ash, it is no more, the linden there is no more, the rate is no more, the mulberry and the moor are no longer there, the platinum is no longer, the elm although there was the disease and many are dead there are varieties that resist the disease, but are not reintroduced and so even they are no longer there, the horse chestnut also does not there is more, the maples that outside of the National Park There are no more, the holly is no longer, I could consult the books continue but that's enough, and all this disappearance from our woods depends only on having made the forestry to earn more money, and destroy all the ecosystem connected to these trees, and to bushes of plants that in the forestry there are no more, and also animals and insects, they also disappear from that environment no longer having their microhabitat, so butterflies wild bees and other insects of which I do not know the name, they can also be extinguished, also animals like the lynx, birds like the oriole, the hawks, the buzzards are not seen anymore, instead animals and birds living from the trash of man increase, such as the crows the seagulls the starlings, etc.

For me the destruction of the land of our country passes through the forestry.

Jesus'

Jesus is back, this year he is 33 years old.

He was born 33 years ago in a barge of African refugees who from North Africa arrived in Sicily, his mother she was nine months pregnant and in the voyage on the barge cause the discomfort broke the waters and bore this child who was given the name Jesus. The mother came from the center of Africa to reach her husband in southern Italy, a man who used to craft the farmhand to collect fruit or tomatoes, in short to collect all the fruits from the earth, a life very honest but made of misery and much effort, he dwelt in a shack made sheet recovered from the abandoned bins containing any pollutant or not, in the summer inside it was a great heat and in winter it trembled from the cold, without electric current and only of gas cookers to cook, to sleep they had torn and very dirty blankets, a mattress found in the dumpster of the filthy that sent a bad smell anyway better this that nothing.

In short they had a great misery, very few moneys that Joseph, father of Jesus, was able to earn served to eat and to send to school Jesus, a very clever and good child, however many times he was teased and also beaten by his classmates, because he was a child of color and because of where he lived It also sent a slight odor. In his class there was also a child son of an industrialist who had many employees in short a powerful man; His son Judas who went to school with Jesus, was a bully boy, hated the people of color and the poor, he loved instead the rich and the mighty.

Jesus grew up and began to love the poor people discarded by the industrial society where it only counts who is well and who has so much money, he learned to love nature and had made friends with a baby mouse who wandered the shack where he lived, he found the company also of a stray dog, a little bastard and very lively a real playful.

Jesus arrived in fifth grade, it happened that the father died for the too hot while it was in fields to collect the tomatoes, therefore the mother took her son and returned to Africa, though where they lived there was the war.

Jesus grew and taught what little he had learned to read and write to other people. The more he grew he loved his own people and the place where he lived where so many animals and many species of trees, and when he taught the words that were dearest to him was when he spoke of the forest of his animals and his trees and said: Do not look for heaven or in infinite space, heaven is here with our friends in our environment, with friend trees and animals, and know that in paradise you are already there, and love it and heal it and defend it from those who want to misuse it.

Judas also had grown up, and his hatred for the weakest increased day by day, he had become general of an army of a super power, and was sent, as they say, to put peace between the two peoples who lived in the nation of Jesus.

Jesus that year he fulfilled thirty-three years, when the army of Judah arrived at his village, Jesus was at school to teach what love the life of any living being and above all our lives, since we have only one, Judas loaded the cannon with a bomb at the depleted uranium and shot it against that school, killing all those who were there.

The story ends here without any winner but all losers.

The crazy and the normal

If there were no crazies the ordinary people did not exist, and then who It would be the normal one, the head of a great super power that wars the whole world to dominate it, or that head of state that with its power puts all its people to hunger to enrich themselves and make the dictator, or even that person who goes to see the football game and he put to cry if his team loses one to zero, I'll tell you: ordinary people do not exist, they just think they are.

The Crazy: crazy people exist I can confirm it, but today they want to make switch to crazy even the thugs who kill people, but it is not so the real crazy does not give boredom to anyone indeed are more sensitive people of so normal, they have fear talking about offending someone, they are quiet to see the lives of others who are well while to them this is denied, it causes his illness, the real lunatics are not bad, they just need someone who loves them, so they don't ask for anything else.

Often poorly seen or seen with fear as if they could do harm to someone, and so the mentally ill are dismissed and mocked if they have a behavior or do something bizarre.

Anyway who feels essay is the real fool.

I because of life: living or dying.

Because this is the thought of a depressive maniac.

- Because life to certain people is so willing to do so many things, and to other illness and misery.
- Because health cannot be bought as many other things but the one who touches is fortunate and who does not touch is unfortunate.
- Because in life there are those who are satisfied with what he has and there are those who are never happy and want more and more, going sometimes even against the law.
- Because there are the clever ones who always make the accounts come back for themselves and there are the foolish that always touches them to do the donkeys.

- Because there are those who have a lot of money and there are those who do not even have money to eat.
- Because there are those who love nature and instead there are those who want to destroy it to make a profit.
- Because there are those who love their lives and others, and instead there are soldiers who kill legally.

Life is full of because without a logical response or equality between the people, maybe this is the ugly of the world in which you live.

The money

The money, they don't look in the face nobody, has them in his hand the rich spends them and after a minute the tramp have them, three pennies, spends and in a second he's holding the tax evader that not hge pays the taxes and in a blink of an eye he has the financier if he spends them, and at a time he has them in his hand the miser that if he holds them tight a little and arrives the heir that if he spends them all and immediately because they do not sweat, and at a time has them in his hand the punter who If you play them all at the gambling and pass in the hands of the mafia that spends them and arrive in hand to the farmer of narcotic plants, who pays taxes and pass in the hands of the cop who he buys cigarettes and also spends it on the doctor who gives it to a junkie who goes to bed with a homosexual who takes the money and makes alms to a priest, who sends them on offer to a country in the third world which government buys weapons and pass in the hands of the manufacturer of arms, which gives the tangent to the governor who pays the fine to the judge who honestly gives them to the government that pays the pensioner who puts them aside and buys food, pays the medicine the bills and the money is finished.

In short, the money does not look at anyone's face, they turn around and pass in the hands of all.

But it would be nice that everyone would give the usual value, the one and only of printed paper, and instead for the money you kill, you discuss among relatives instead of wanting well, do you race to those who has of more and who is richer not looking in the face of no one from where the money, the illegal or legal, in short to the money we give a value that they do not have, certainly it takes to live, but when enough you have to settle.

The Real Heroes

Who are the heroes, people who go to battle to fight enemies, but enemies of those, people you don't even know if they are good or bad, if they have family with children like you, but you have to shoot them anyway because they have a different uniform from your, or the real enemies are those who govern us, their rulers always ready to make tyrants if the people do not obey taxes and laws imposed.

Surely the real heroes are not the soldiers of any army are, but they are the ordinary people that every day they stand quietly and go to work all day long, often a tiring and poorly paid job, just enough to span the family. Already the workers the last wheel of the wagon, but ready with their work to make rich a nation, people who just ask to live in peace with all, these are the real heroes,

heroes every day for the whole life without a medal without being saints.

The workers the many saints of everyday that when they die have a miserable funeral, yes, because even that coast and money there are never enough, few people because in society did not count much and so there are relatives and some close friends and away without a memory of anything.

The Love

The most beautiful thing for a couple is fidelity and friendship, because love the physical one then passes but the remaining faithful and friends lasts all life, unfortunately many couples leave and I think they suffer a lot as a sense of abandonment.

In a couple the first thing to get along is to want with all the maybe stay together even when life takes you to be more arrogant you have to have one of the two let go of the words, and think that after all passes and returns normal to want well. The past life alone is a lost life thrown into the trash, instead being together with another person fills you with the heart of joy, you can talk about your most intimate things, you can express your thoughts freely and discuss it without decency, we were born to live in two.

Many people turn around the world to look for the soul mate and do not realize that instead you have to give love to receive it as well, and perhaps whoever loves you is closer than you think.

The Hunger

In watching television sometimes I'm ashamed to see poorly fed children that they often die of hunger, I fat like a pig, perhaps due to the psychotropic drugs that I take, I have a sense of guilt because I eat a lot but I cannot do without it.

But the shame that I feel should not be just mine but also the wealthiest states of food that should help not with money but with groceries the poorest nations, because it is useless to send money because those do not eat but they go to make enrich only those who manage them.

This poverty is often due to climatic factors, but it is often due to the wars of the rulers of those places that either for oil or other riches such as gold precious stones or mines of elements that serve to send the nuclear power plants of the richest countries, in short, every pretext is good to keep those poor people in misery and hunger.

Let's give him food instead of money we lose tractors instead of weapons we lose drills to dig wells for water instead of drills to dig oil that so much goes to finish everything to the richest nations we lose people who teach him in schools instead of the military of our countries with the falsehood of saying that they bring peace, let them doctors, instead of the hidden objects that are ready to plunder that little wealth has remained, help materially and hunger may be defeated.

The freedom

Freedom, where freedom is, what freedom is, what makes us feel free.

The freedom for us mentally ill in the past there was also denied physically, enclosed in the asylums because people were afraid of us and we had to spend the whole life or the luckiest healed and so they could go out. For normal people freedom was perceived as participating in all social events by the municipalities to reach the state, or participate in the laws of the state with demonstrations and strikes. But so one is just a number of the many who participate because it does not say its point of view, in my opinion the real freedom is to put black on white the own opinions the own thoughts, right or wrong that they are, and for a mentally ill this is just a record if you think about the past when we were locked up in the asylums. The freedom to express itself is something that must always be defended by those who want to silence with laws and power.

Write to be able to publish their opinions also against those who raise the voice and who is angry with us or drag us to court, THIS IS THE REAL FREEDOM.

My illness

It's been two days that I feel bad, but today it is even stronger the desire to die, you never leave your thoughts the desire to kill you.

I took 25 drops of En and I feel slowly a relaxation, although certain thoughts of dying in part remain, the distress the inner discomfort those are going away, and then reappearing finished the effect of the drops of this medicine.

I take so many psychotropic drugs and it is ugly to go up and down with the mood, it is very bad, although I do not miss anything, I miss the most, "the Health ".

Thanks to my sister who helps me by giving me a salary although because of this disease I do not work every week, I can keep my family, thanks Cinzia.

Every passing year I realize that mental illness worsens, mood swings are sharper and closer to one another, up and down, always so every week, and sometimes even the usual day, it is tremendous the pain that you try, the memory is going away, no longer remember the names of the people you have to think as you call a person you know, but you often don't remember at all.

My brain is frying by all the medicines I take, and the fear that one day does not make it more to keep the family tortures me the conscience, but what can I do if this brain abandons me every day more.

But what can I do if every morning when I wake up I find myself having to climb over a wall so high that you can't do it, and you get the anguish, the anxiety that makes you take a knot in the throat that you can't send down.

Hopefully in the future the situation of my brain better but after taking different types of psychotropic drugs are a little pessimist, however hope is the last to die.

The Industrial society

The industrial society of the richest nations is based on consumerism, the more you consume the more work there is the more workers are paid the more they can consume, the less they are paid less consume and the industries year less work.

If wealth gathers in a few people, slowly they will become poorer because their industries will have less work then less gain. A nation where it pays its workers little, is a nation reduced to impoverishing year after year.

The Government of a state should be like a person's brain, directing his own body in the interests of things that are worth more for the person and well-being, so a government must drive its people to a common well-being, and not a few people who govern the people and a circle of industrial or wealthy compliant.

The welfare of a people is about many things, but the most important is the environment in which it lives, city or countryside. Respect the environment should be the first thing they teach in a school, to recognize animals, insects, reptiles, trees, herbs and flowers at the very least of their nation, do not teach this equates to dismiss the interest from the world around us, and that is why today many people are attracted more by electronic objects, than by the recognize a chestnut from an oak tree. So you are losing the value of what surrounds us, and walking in a forest there by no feeling because we lost nature contact and the song of a nightingale can be mistaken for the song of a blackbird.

The white man

Bo I do not know why the white man treats the nature in which he lives as something to plunder, something that is beneficial to him to take change model to his own pleasure and gain, and does not treat those who live there as something precious to have to save and protect, and model him to the environment where he wants to live, instead, the indigenous people of other continent have done.

I live in a valley where nature was all shaped to needs of the white man, was made all forestry, all chestnut to feed the people before the industrialization all oaks to heat the houses, all beech to make wood for paper and high trunk for timber and fir trees for lumber, pinewoods to reclaim the stony land, fields to cultivate grain and other essences then some abandoned with the arrival of the industries, in short everything or to the needs of the white man, the imagination of leaving also the other plants less useful but not for this less important for the environment in which you live, so these plants removed from the woods are often found in the gardens or also to form avenues in public and private land.

Mental illness

Who are the mentally ill and what many people think if he asks.

The mentally ill are like clouds in the sky ready to change thought to every breath of wind, unsure of their thoughts walk without a fixed goal, ready to ask for a cigarette smoking to kill the time, you recognize them for their bizarre behavior because they are stuffed with drugs, they often fail to work and so they are to the margin of society.

Alone without the love of a possibly normal woman are found to see as spectators the lives of other normal people with car money and women, all that is missing to them.

Often who is not cared for and followed by the doctors, he finds himself sleeping under the bridges with his own delirium or depression. I was lucky, because or found a good wife, she married me despite my psychic sickness, and we have two beautiful little girls. A friend of mine instead was normal when marrying, had bought the house, had two beautiful girls, then arrived the monster the mental illness, within a few years the disease has gone worse and so to lost all house wife and girls, who sold the house the wife took the money and the girls and she went away.

We are not

- We are neither puppets nor fools,
- We are neither guinea pigs nor chemical experiments,
- We are not dangerous if cured,
- We are not the object of mockery because we are sick,
- We are not the nothing because we also exist and think,
- We are not unable to do anything because we also work for what we can,
- We are not callous because we also love,

- We are not strong and indestructible because we are human too,
- We are not heroes nor great people because we are weaker,
- We are not gods because we are people,
- We are neither devils nor witches,
- We are not spiteful because we also respect others,
- We are not the same people as the others but we are more sensitive,
- We are not weights for society but we give what we can,
- We are nothing more than the others but we are only mentally ill.

Passage without return

In life, it is a walk without return.

We marry to be in company in this world of solitude, without wife is a life lost thrown to the wind, we strive in the search for something that we do not or that does not exist yet to satisfy our being nothing in front of the mass of people who exist in this planet.

Being someone who counts at the social level, puts us in a race for those who has more, more money more homes more power on other people, in short it is a race that last a lifetime until the death; and so we close ourselves inside the factories or other buildings to work as if the only aim is that to produce more and more we do not notice that we are throwing away all the existence on this planet.

Life in the cities and the hectic work we used to distract us from the wonder of what exists in this world, so the countless varieties of life plant animals fish mushrooms and insects end up not being known or known by chance only in a small part.

Peoples

I was a child I had 7-8 years of age and my father taught me to fish with the cane in the river, so for sport. Fishing the fish gradually learned to recognize the species that were in the river, and to respect them, and with the respect parts the love for these fish, and stopped to fish them.

At the age of 18, I took the driving license, and so he did not need to eat, but for sport I was hunting, I killed free animals to eat them but although I did not need it because to eat I had it already. I learned to recognize them specie by species, to respect them and with respect there was love, so stopped to go hunting and after I was so sorry to have killed these animals.

Today I don't know if this my theory of recognizing people for human people and to respecting them brings this respect to love among people even so different, I do not know.

I'm just a fool who would want an unattainable thing, bringing peace in the world with words and dialogue among peoples, putting aside hostilities with arms, but deepening knowledge among peoples that quarrels understand the customs of both, the eating the dress what is most at heart to every people, then respect all the political ideas of each country and so that with respect for the ideas of others is born the love also between different peoples, and is precisely the diversity of ideas that enriches this planet, from a planet seen in a whole same way monotonous and ugly.

I do not delude myself that with this writing I can solve something, however I really think that with knowledge and respect can born love also among different peoples culturally.

Prayer

Dear Jesus forgive me because I love flowers,

Jesus forgive me because I love trees,

Jesus forgive me because I love birds flying in the sky,

Jesus forgive me because I love all the animals,

Jesus forgive me because I love fish

Jesus forgive me because I love insects even the most venomous

Jesus forgive me because I love reptiles from the crocodile to the smallest of reptiles,

Jesus forgive me because I love water and fire,

Jesus forgive me because I love the pure air that I breathe,

Jesus forgive me because I love the world in which I live.

Jesus forgive me because every day with the chainsaw I shoot trees,

Jesus forgive me because every day peaches prunes of fish and many are thrown into the dead Sea,

Jesus forgive me because every day I go hunting for wild animals often to get them near the extinction,

Jesus forgive me because my way of life in civilized person creates so many wastes that pollute air water rivers seas land with landfills,

Jesus forgive me because with my presumption of being superior throwing missiles and bombs of all kinds pollutants or not,

Jesus forgive me because with my intelligence I have come to build atomic powerhouses and atomic bombs that are blown up in the open air and with the breaking of nuclear power plants have helped to make our world more radioactive causing the increase of tumors,

Jesus forgive me because I am destroying your PARADISE

Antonio Piantini

Spring

Winter ends the air buys a pleasant warmth, the first to realize are the animals especially the birds that with their chirping cheer the air in a romantic harmony that makes open the heart to those who want to love indiscriminately both people and nature.

The plants awaken from the winter hibernation, the buds begin to swell and then giving birth to beautiful flowers, nectar for many insects.

They begin to have the first fruits of the vegetable garden flavored because fresh and sighed after so much sweat fatigue. As the days pass by, the air becomes warmer and the first fruits of the trees come, the cherries are among the first, colored sweets of a beautiful bright red that says eat immediately.

Begin to be born the mushrooms, the prugnoli are among the first, fragrant good to make us the pasta.

In the spring you want to go for walks in the sun with some friends or someone love and the flowers of the fields attract our attention and the curiosity, we stop to look at them always as it was the first time.

A world, an image

- Imagine a world of good people.
- Imagine a world where there are no weapons.
- Imagine a world where there are no wars imagine a world where people want well.
- Imagine a world where people help themselves in work the one with the other.
- Imagine a world where there is the love for all things created by God.
- Imagine a world where there is no money.
- Imagine a world where there are no tyrants.

- Imagine a world where nature retakes the Earth from the man abandoned.
- Imagine a world where all peoples want to be well.
- Imagine a world where you don't kill wild animals.
- Imagine a world that the man only eats from animals or fish bred by him.
- Imagine a world where a tree is worth more than a hundred bricks.
- Imagine a world where diseases are cured at all.
- Imagine a world where people don't die more than hunger.
- Imagine a world made of love.

Who is a gentleman

A gentleman is surely one who is content with what he has, who likes the work he does and draws satisfaction every day more from what he can do again with your own means without having to resort to mortgages or loans from anyone.

A gentleman is definitely one who likes to help others, surely he can be a doctor, a nurse, who help the sick every day, while receiving a small salary compared to what they do.

Can be a gentleman even those who behave honestly with others, do not cheat them nor to tease them.

A gentleman is not said to be dressed for strength with jacket and tie, but can also be an Amazon's indigenous that respects and protects the environment in which it lives, does not destroying for except cash profit because it attracted by the technology and the junk of the white man.

A gentleman is definitely one who he is in peace with himself and he doesn't always run behind what you don't it can come, but he lives a happy life even with a euro in his pocket.

Fantasy

- Use fantasy to see all the people in the world dressed in pink.
- Use fantasy to see a world where there are no weapons but bouquets of flowers.
- Use fantasy to see a world without deserts but full of trees.
- Use fantasy to free yourself in the air and fly up and wish your life to all the birds that no longer die under the shooting of the hunters.
- Use fantasy to become a laundry network so that the fish return free to the sea from alive and not from the dead.

- Use fantasy to be a bomber who can't drop bombs on people's houses but he touches them back to the base.
- Use the fantasy to have an eraser so big that you can erase all the diseases of the world.
- Use fantasy to feed all the living beings of the earth and not to starve any more.
- Use fantasy to be a hero who gets up every day and goes to work humbly to feed and keep his family.
- Use the imagination to make a little effort every day to improve your life and that of all.

Living a Life

The life of a person, handicapped or not, should be a joy to stay in the world and no a race for those who has plus, like who Govern the state or any public body take advantage of its own charge to take more money possibly cheating, or legally with exaggerated wages, or as many individuals who evade as much as possible the tax, or worse still make money by polluting the environment with abusive landfills or pouring directly into the rivers toxic and noxious substances.

Life is not this.

A person's life should have other ideals, for example, to enjoy life day after day, working less hours than the current 8 hours but working 6 hours or less, but working all without unemployed or case integration people but have the chance to choose the job you like the most and not the one that by chance is more paid or what happens, however don't like it.

The state should guarantee to all: housewives who dedicate themselves to the family, workers of any work they do, sick of any chronic illness or not, an equal salary for all because in life we have the right to live worthily all without seeking alms to anyone, then more money have all more consumption there is and so much more work for everyone.

Capitalism

Capitalism, the infernal machine that with its technology and its hunger to consume every what's on this planet It makes us all guilty (none excluded), of the disappearance of several animal and plant species.

The life of man is not in my opinion very beautiful, with the illusion that money creates well-being, life for many it is a race to those who do more and then try to have more power over other people. In this unbridled race to those who possess more (houses, car, boats, land, televisions, computer, etc.), You do not look in the face of anyone, so for money and power you build increasingly destructive weapons to kill more and more people in the name progress and freedom from dictatorships, no more compliant with the new stronger nations and dictator of the planet.

If capitalism and so said well-being will come to the whole planet, to get more out of nature, especially the animal and plant species that have less interest for man.

The richness of the few and the poverty of many, unemployed, sick, disabled civilians and labor, pensioners with the minimum, workers of the industry and other, people who every day have to reckon with the few moneys they have, people who if they feel bad they have to choose whether to eat or treat this is the true poverty of capitalism, while the real rich want more and more consumerism to keep alive and flourished their activities.

So it cannot go long before the planet Earth, or the people rebel.

Life, should be a joy for all living beings, from birth to death, especially for man should be a guarantee of assistance from all (i.e. the state), for all, from the weakest of health or other to the strongest.

Instead of increasing consumerism, to always enrich the usual scoundrels, we increase this wealth of manpower that we have in addition to helping weaker beings, man and other living beings, to decrease working hours (if there is too much production in that sector), helping especially the elderly, that after a lifetime spent working often they are in the house alone, and loneliness is the ugliest disease feeling abandoned by everyone even if the children come to see you once a week.

To my Major

Mr. Mayor, I am your citizen who would like to propose an idea that would in the time of 20 \ 30 years a good tourism in our municipality and more passes the time more will become famous and more people will come to see it. My proposal and to build the largest giant Sequoias park in Europe, only 2000 plants are enough to be the first park in Europe. I could provide all the seedlings ready to be planted in the chosen place, giving to the municipality just to do a great thing in our small town. Of course the park must be done in the municipality of Castel San Niccolò. Now the first European Sequoias Park is in Germany on the border with the Netherlands, with a number of giant sequoias equal to 1500 specimens, planted in the year 1952.

In Italy the largest park of Sequoias is in Reggello province of Florence with a number of 100 Giant Sequoias.

The Sequoias are surely the most known tree in the world both for their thickness, and for its longevity, equal to 3200/3.500 years; it seems that the older sequoias saw the birth of several pharaohs in Egypt.

Making a park so in our municipality is like taking it in the first places in the tourist level and in the first places at public parks level. The giant Sequoia has a rapid growth and as a climatic zone the best is towards Cetica it holds to -30 degrees below zero and as a young man is really beautiful, Mr.

Mayor, I Antonio seedlings the invitation to see it at the factory where we produce wooden floors, the sequoia that or planted in the 1982 was small 20 \ 30 cm and is now beautiful.

I in my life or made birth about 1.200 giant Sequoias, half of them I've already given them to friends who love trees, a little bit takes the town of Vignola (that of cherries) with other plants such as: the Metasequoia, the Taxodium, the Ginkgo biloba, all plants that I do to give them, and a reason there is why I do it,

THEY ARE ALL PLANTS VULNERABLE AND SUBJECT TO EXTINCTION

The other half of giant sequoias I still have them in the box, where they are born, will be about 500 \ 600 seedlings and grow very well, there are those who have already asked me all, but I would prefer to give them to my municipality.

The seeds I got through a wholesaler directly from America, not only of Sequoia giant, but also of other plants, such as Taxodium (Bald Cypress) and Sequoia Sempervirens.

My friend to whom I gifted more giant sequoias of all about 400 is happy to leave something important after his death, something that you remember for a long time of what he did in life to plant thousand trees and hopes to have an economic return even as soon as the plants will be a little older.

Giant Sequoias do not have an economic market for sale, there is no demand for nurseries by people, perhaps because they do not have big gardens, or they think they cannot live here in our climate, told me the nurseryman Brogi L. brother of the most known L. Brogi, who since he opened the nursery he sold only one and it is ten years that opened it.

With this does not mean that people remain indifferent because as soon as we talk about these plants (the sequoias) people are fascinated that they can live here, and asks where they can see them in large numbers, I generally say the most beautiful are in Vallombrosa in the wood and they are about 130 years old.

Another place is in Reggello where there are 100 specimens.

Anyway if my idea was taken into consideration from you, the most competent person to realize the project in my opinion is my friend L. Brogi very skilled in building gardens and parks as well as deep connoisseur of trees, bushes and flowers etc. etc.

Kind regards

Antonio Piantini.

The Davidia

The Davidia or tree of handkerchiefs, is a plant little known but of remarkable beauty, with its two petals correctly called bracts long 12 \ 25 cm. About, a shorter (12 cm.) and a longest (25 cm.), completely white pure characterize the beauty and name of this plant. The flowering remains hanging on the tree from fifteen to thirty days, and the bracts grow on average 1 cm per day.

The flowering of this tree takes place after several years about ten, so either you buy a plant of several years or if the plant is small, you have to have a little patience. The tree growth is fast and reaches considerable size about 20 meters of height, the plant from small loves to be watered when the season is drier, and wants a soil very rich in loam, in winter loses the leaves and it can resist to the cold climate of almost all the Europe. I have at home one that flowered me in 2010 and I must say that the wait of eight years for the first flowering has been remarkably repaid.

Mushrooms

I for those who do not know me are Antonio Piantini born October 7th 1965, since 1993 I am in psychiatric care at the Institute of Health and Mental Hygiene, also called S.I.M. of Bibbiena at the USL of Bibbiena station.

My psychic disorder is called: Bipolar mood syndrome (or as it was called first depressive manic disorder) The name itself is scary, it causes the bad talk of journalists of crime episodes attributed, without a psychiatrist's opinion, to depressive maniacs, without calculating that many people have this psychic disorder and make a life almost completely normal.

In my life the personality disorder called schizzotipico appeared soon, after finishing the middle school I withdrew from society more and more, contributing to the fact that I worked in my father's factory next to our house. My hobbies were (always to stay isolated): fishing and mushroom research, in these two hobbies or learned to recognize many species of mushrooms and many varieties of freshwater fish, a 18 years taken both the driving license and the hunting license. Hunting I liked especially the hunt for the blackbird and the jay because I used to go for long walks in the meadows and in the woods, perhaps more than hunting was that the real fun, with the hunt I learned to recognize so many animals and birds, and then to love them and stop hunting.

In the years I went hunting I had a Breton female puppy dog mixed Setter, the puppy grew and I took her with me on the hunt, but she was afraid of the shooting, many told me to give her away because there would be no remedy, but I with patience and with love the fear will took it however after a short time, as I already said above I learned to love animals and stopped the hunt, I was alone with the only fun company, my small dog Mina; the hunt I had stopped, fishing also because I did not like to stand still, I had remained the look for mushrooms, thing that I still liked, and the dog that make it? Give it away or no! Because I was fond of her, then what to do to make her want well in the family? I teach her looking for mushrooms, but not all mushrooms, only porcini mushrooms. Often you went myself and my mother seek mushrooms with Mina always found many, there was a period I was leaving with the car in the evening after five I went to the mountain with the dog, and I went home at eight thirty nine o'clock with a basket full of porcini mushrooms, the thing followed for a month, a few months after the psychosis arrived, and lost contact with reality I didn't want the meds and I was getting worse, until after two months of delirium I accepted the medicine from my sister and then I realized my illness and I always cared, although it is difficult to send down to be mentally ill especially when people do not consider you anything.

Our planet

I do not know what to think today my brain passes by pole in bough does not stop to make a logical reasoning, perhaps the reduction of medicines a little hasty caused this disruption, I feel very anymore, however I try to say something I think.

Everyone in life we have dreams that we would like to realize, who would like a house of its own, in case isolated with a beautiful garden, or a beautiful partner or mate to stay together all life, or even a beautiful car or bike, in short we all have dreams that a made, they fade because they are already made and are no longer so desired as before.

But dreams do not end because they appear of others, and so throughout their lives.

It was this that in the hundred has made the spring of capitalism in the west and still together with the human inventiveness creates well-being to our populations.

But dreams are sometimes not enough to create well-being if getting back is the environment in which we live, we must create a balance, hard to do where the man lives in the well-being, but with much respect for the forests of the rivers of the lakes of the fields of others around, before blame other states of continents far from ours for the destruction of the ecological equilibrium of our planet.

The earth belongs to all we make good use.

Lamberto

Life sometimes is short for everything we want to achieve, for what we do what we care more and make finished, to never regret having a thousand things to do and are all through.

The first time I saw so many giant sequoias very little, I saw them by my friend Lamberto, he will have had about 200, someone I bought it to give it to friends and nurses of psychiatric center.

One day as the redwoods were not sold, to create space in the nursery the cousin of Lamberto threw them away, I went to the nursery to buy some more, but his cousin told me he threw them in the bed of the river, I went straight to see, and with my regret had really thrown them away, I went back to the nursery and I made jars to try to recover as much as possible, I returned to the bed of the river and I immediately started to repot as much as possible filling the door rack of the car, I went home to empty it and then I return to get more the whole is repeated until the sequoias were in good state of preservation.

It was there in seeing these small plants of trees so immense that I came up with the idea of realizing something as big as they are: the first park of giant sequoias in Europe.

The plants that I saved I made to grow and I all gave them, I gave also to my friend Lamberto who had made them born and planted in his farm.

To build this park of sequoias you had to know where to take the seeds, I asked my friend Lamberto since he the seeds had already bought them, he gave me the name of the company and I bought about 30 grams, they grew about 600 sequoias, the ground to put so many plants I didn't indeed I still had to buy and every year meanwhile the plants grew, fortunately or destiny wanted that Lamberto met a woman who made farm to which she really like trees, and immediately liked the idea of making a park of giant sequoias, according to the terrain she had, we made the bill that there could stay about 400, I all gave to her, however It will become the first Italian park of giants Sequoia, not European, my goal will be to participate instead to make the first European Sequoias parch here in Casentino possible in my municipality.

A Maria

Dear Maria the first time I saw you I remember that the Gerini brought you with his car there at the shop, and I was out in the square so much so that you wouldn't even come down from the car, I saw you through the windows already because I was from the opposite side of where you were, I liked you immediately with that indescribable face from how beautiful you had reddish hair that gave you so beauty. We decided then to go out together to get to know each other better, I thought to myself that with a girl so beautiful I had never come out. The meeting as agreed was to the gardens in front of the elementary School in Ponte a Poppi, our first outing ended with a big chat, but we realized that it was good together and so another appointment was fixed. The time after turning with the car at some point I asked her if she gave me a kiss, she replied of yes, I stopped with the car in a pitch and we kissed: was a beautiful kiss, I began to understand that the two of us were just fine together.

It passed so many years but that kiss I remember it again, more time passes and more increases the love for my wife, I had so much luck that day to meet her.

There would be so many other things to tell, but it will be for another time.

Plants

In the lives of people each of us have particular interests or hobbies that make us feel made and happy for that we do.

I Antonio Piantini, I am a carpenter by trade, craftsman on his own, and as a hobby I like to sow and
104

bring birth trees that are vulnerable to extinction as: The *Sequoiadendron Giganteum* and Sequoia *Sempervirens,* severely threatened with extinction as the *Redwood,* in addition to the threatened extinction, the *Ginkgo Biloba.*

However, I do not only give birth to these trees, but also others such as: *Taxodium,* beautiful tree that however He needs a ditch with water near, *Pinus L.* which is the highest pine and the largest in diameter of all pines. In 2009 was also born *The Eucalyptus Gunnì* that has withstood the winter 2009 \ 2010 with temperature -18°c.

In the Spring 2010 was born 500 \ 600 about *SequoiaDendron,* I call them my girls, when one dries my heart cries and I always think it could be her to become millennial. In my life I am forty-five years old and with the great help of my wife, P. Maria A. we have been born about 1.200 *SequoiaDendron*, we found to present them almost all, to people who really care about trees.

Anyway I have to thank my friend B. Lamberto and Silvia. L. who accepted my idea of doing the park of *Sequoiadendron* largest in Italy here in Casentino.

My dream would be to make in Italy the largest giant Sequoias park in Europe, (because now the primacy is expected in Germany with the number of 1.500 *Sequoiadendron*), of course I would like to participate too, giving birth and growing the seedlings until are ready to be planted definitively, doing this for free. ONLY TO MAKE A SMALL CONTRIBITION TO SAVE TREES VULNERABLE TO EXTICTION.

Kings and Queens

Maybe it takes a little or a lot of madness I don't know in sowing plants that have no market, not even if gifts. Yet you have to hope that someone is interested in the life of these rare trees often unknown, yet beautiful with elegant doorways worthy of kings and queens.

The plant that fascinates me the most and surely the Giant Sequoia, for the first two giant redwoods I worked a whole day in a wooden roof. The plants were very small high about 20 \ 30cm, my father PIANTINI RINO (also he, lover of the trees) gave me two places to put them, one near a ditch and the other in the midst of hazelnuts, were planted in 1982. Now they are very big, for me that I love trees is a big satisfaction.

God is there

- If allowed me to be born God is there.
- If he gave me a father and a mother God exists.
- If there is food for everyone God exists
- If the sun lights up all the houses God exists
- If trees give oxygen to all living beings God exists.
- If the flowers come both in the gardens of the rich and the poor God exists.
- If there are animals and fish God exists.
- If allowed me to have a wife God exists.
- If He gave me a family God exists.
- If he will make me die according to his will God exists.

Metasequoia

It is evening and I begin to have sleep, perhaps the fault of the psychotropic drugs that I take, however I still don't want to go to bed, if I don't talk about a tree that is very much at heart, the *Redwood*.

The Tree of *Redwood* It is like a puppy of a very rare dog that mother nature abandoned to remain a miserable number of 100 specimens in China.

In the 1940s \ 50 was discovered, and distributed the seeds in Europe and America, and to avoid the extinction it made a restocking of 5.400 specimens. There are also small groves of about 30 specimens.

To me would like that every person who makes a garden, with an ample space and soil type compatible with the *Redwood*, be adopted as you do with a puppy a "*Redwood*".

Its leaves are soft velvety as the hair of a kitten, its color is of light green, its growth is rapid and in a few years it is a tree of considerable size. The leaves in autumn fall and before falling change in color assuming a beautiful reddish yellow color.

Lapis Dot

I in this planet are just a dot of lapis, but I think: I have the brain sick it takes several psychotropic drugs to make it stand on the roadway, but I can think.

I think man has not yet understood how beautiful diversity is: from man to man, from race to human race, from species to animal species, between varieties of plants and fish, but continues to manipulate the planet according to its own consumption, so animal and plant species and unfortunately also human races with less economic interest are discarded , as if they were rubbish, or enclosed in small ghettos or places only to preserve the species, instead according to me diversity is the true richness of the earth and the tourist man of this planet in the near future will have to give you more and more value, because with the speed of budge that exists today, tourism the true richness of tomorrow will want to see more and more the natural beauty of the animal and plant varieties present in those places, possibly not touched by man or at least restored as if they were natural.

The banks

The banks, strange shops, where they accumulate paper and numbers, sellers of illusions and smoke where one feels rich or poor according to the numbers deposited. Rich or poor but of that? Of a cold thing, the money not certain of affections that you change based on the money paid into the account, money that does not belong to anyone but lies them cold and motionless ready to be picked up to every need. Demanded by all in exaggerated quantity, the money the banks offer it to everyone in pledge of your assets, and so one will deposes of precious goods to have in quantity to make a good life, and the banks are fattened by the loss of the goods of others.

Banks unconscious custodians of happiness or sadness, everything runs around them wealth or poverty, luck or misfortune to have a nice nest in the account or be indebted to them.

I love

I love diversity in plants as in animals is this the true richness of this planet, I am just a passenger who admires this wealth and tries to lend a hand to those who remain a little behind in the competitiveness of reproduction

Each of us who passes on this planet tries to do something that remains in time more or less long, to be remembered by the next generation.

Men with more power both political and economic leave in general with the help of architects, painters and sculptors more imposing and fascinating works. The most common people, who she has to work all day to span, she relies on hobbies to create something that is particular and possibly lasts long in time, among them I am too.

My hobby in particular is sowing giant sequoias make them grow two or three years and then give them to friends or even to people who like plants.

To be born The *Sequoiadendron giganteum* is a thing that always makes me shivers for emotion and great joy, to think that small seedlings can someday become gigantic trees and I was the one to make them born, the thing fills me with joy.

For now, my wife and I talking we born about 1.200 seedlings, half have already been given the others were born in the spring 2010 still are small to be planted will still have to wait two years in pot.

The life of the giant sequoias is very long, between 3200 and 3500 years almost like the tombs of the last Egyptian pharaohs.

"PLANTING A SEQUOIA IN A PERSON' S LIFE EQUATES TO BUILDING A PYRAMID WITHOUT HOWEVER MAKING ANY SLAVE".

Planet Earth

Di Piantini Antonio

Life ahead man

It was a beautiful planet, full of life both in the waters and in the earth, wax many species of fish and many species of animals, life was that the strongest eats the weakest, but the animals were kept in equilibrium, the herbivores if they increased in number also increased the carnivores and thus decreased the herbivores, and also the carnivores diminished.

The balance was thus maintained for millennia and so was also happening in the sea that if it increased a species of fish, it also increased its predators, until they returned to a pre-existing equilibrium.

This planet had immense forests of trees, there lived every kind of tree in its ideal climate, they wax trees that lived where it was hotter and those who lived where it was colder. The climate was pleasant, however, in the millennia it varied, from the times it increased the cold, increasing the glaciers, and from the times it increased the heat of melting a part of the glaciers.

Life was beautiful and so it had been for thousands of years until slowly a kind of animal was getting smarter up to excel on other living species, until he had the complete dominion of the planet. Was the man.

The history of man

The man stands out immediately from the other species for the aggression, who had for its similar as on the animals. The story of man up to the year two thousand and even further, is marked by wars and murders, as if the only the purpose of the rulers of each people is to kill their fellows to dominate as many people as possible.

And even today the history of the man is of those who make wars or suppress their own people to tyrannize and remain in power as a dictator.

Man this being thinking that with his intelligence to revolutionized with technology his way of life to be superior on other beings living, but has not yet understood that he is living on what defines the church as the terrestrial paradise.

It's just so this planet is our paradise, and as such it must be defended by those who are destroying it, but not by making further wars, but it must be defended with the love, making it clear to its rulers that history should no longer be written by those who make wars, but by whom with the love protects any living being of the planet Earth.

The wars that stupid thing, to destroy with bombs all that God and The man have created.

The Terrestrial Paradise

Paradise is our planet Earth, with its infinite animals starting from the whale and the elephant two animals one master of the seas and the other master of the Earth, two gigantic and so fascinating beings, who unfortunately risk the extinction.

Among the birds surely the most fascinating is the eagle for its mighty stature and openness of wings.

Among the insects surely the most significant are the butterflies, wonderful for their variety and beauty for the colors of their wings, unfortunately there have been few varieties, for the destruction of their habitat.

Among the fish certainly makes the shark suggestion in all its varieties, even he hunted by man for its danger to swimmers.

Among the reptiles makes more impression surely the crocodile with its huge mouth full of teeth, among the serpents surely the master is the Cobra and the Anaconda one for his poisonousness the other for its coarseness.

Among the plants the mistress is definitely the giant sequoia with its immense thickness and longevity and among the flowers surely the most beautiful is the orchid with its varieties of flowers almost all beautiful. What I wrote here is nothing compared to the varieties that are on our earthly paradise. (*How I love this planet*).

The riches of the Earth

This planet that with the richness of the water, which has given life to all living beings on earth is a wonderful thing and it is a pity that the rivers from the times are taken and used as sewers to open sky.

Anyway the world goes on despite the man does everything to change it to your liking, the fields abandoned by the man floor plan they return woods and nature resembles its cycle.

This planet where inside is the fire that with the volcanoes releases lava reminds us that we live in a world similar to a pressure cooker, with the volcanoes always ready to explode and to bring destruction.

This planet with its climate that varies according to its latitude from the great cold to the great heat, offers life in every climate that has, from the cold that we live penguins to the south and seals and polar bears to the north, until you get to the great heat of the equator where they live a big number of animals and plants.

But the climate because of the man is changing, with pollution greenhouse gases the climate increases in degrees, so the more to suffer is the vegetation that with warming up takes more easily fire, so they go into smoke entire forests of trees, what a shame.

I love this planet

I Antonio Piantini at forty eight years old I must say that I fell in love with this planet Earth, and I suffer a lot when I see that man mistreats him in all its forms, polluting the rivers, or when the man from fire to the woods or the forests , or when it is deforested without replanting, or when they do with landfill waste where it happens in any terrain and not in the appropriate places, or when the man with the hunt arrives to put almost at risk of extinction animal species, or when with the chainsaw puts in risk of extinction trees and other plants, or even when you make forestry with only one species of tree for large extensions, without calculating that this will ruin an entire ecosystem, or when fish are taken and the non-marketable ones are thrown into the dead sea, that waste of food.

I'm sick more when I see poorly nourished children who often die of hunger, who slap in the face to the rich food countries. I'm very ill when I see the wars it does man against their fellows, for any reason in the world this should not happen. Poor planet Earth in what hands are you finished, men who love nothing out of that money and power.

Trees

Di Piantini Antonio

Woods in Italy

Luca was a mentally ill who had put himself in his head, in his delirium, to change the world, but what change of the world?

Change the vision that man a in the world, especially the vision that the man It has on nature and the weakest beings of nature "the trees".

The trees that where Luca lived the woods were all made to forestry i.e. one species of trees for large plots of land, without understanding that in a forest are important all the trees that we can stay in that climate and type of land, because each tree creates a micro habitat where they live with him mushrooms, insects, animals, birds, which feed on the leaves or the fruits, the mushrooms that live in symbiosis with that species of tree. In short, removing from the woods so many species of trees are tantamount to destroying the whole ecosystem of that part of the forest, without thinking that they have the right to live all the trees.

This is the problem here in Italy, and in the rest of the world? ... ...

In the rest of the world the problem and another, the deforestation to make pastures for the cattle, or cut many trees to work a few. What a destruction.

The usefulness of all trees

Explaining to seven billion people living in our planet the importance of the diversity of trees in a forest is not so much easy, but you have to understand that each tree is connected to another living being or perhaps even more than one, each plant offers something, with flowers the nectar to make honey for bees and other insects yet birds like hummingbirds, with the fruits that give so much food to man and many other animals and insects, with the leaves that they are also eaten by animals and insects such as the caterpillars that will turn into beautiful butterflies, with wood, so useful to the man to build houses and other works, for the fire that heats and makes cook man, and each tree offers a different wood from plant to plant having everyone a service, one to make the beams of a house another plant to make doors another type of plant to make floors, another plant has a wood that holds well to the outside you make the fixtures, another type of plant has good wood to burn in the path or in the stove, in short every tree is useful to something, that is why in a forest there must be all the plants that can live there.

Understand this and already a step forward in building a beautiful forest.

My conscience

Luca says: I would simply tell the world to stop for a minute to think about what's more worth, a house full of wood or a forest standing.

I have done the carpenter for thirty-five years and I have worked so much wood, that I do not even know how many forests I have shot down, because, to satisfy the vanity of the people, until one day drowned by the pain of having done so much harm to my planet I did not make it anymore and because of my illness (Manic Depressive Psychosis) and the conscience that screamed in me telling me to stop waste so much wood, so much death of innocent trees because free in the forests, that day I did not make it anymore and I stopped making the carpenter, although still alive of that craft, hopefully in a future can live of what I write, a peaceful craft without giving boredom to anyone just a little bit of paper to open the heart to someone who wants to listen.

I would like in my delirium that those who read these words of mine think a little bit about before buying any wooden object, think about the deforestation that is done to make that piece of wood.

The forests in the world are

dwindling and I no longer want to contribute to this havoc says Luca.

Luca says

Luca says:

each tree that saw is a life that we break.

Luca says:

each branch that saw is a torture that, we inflict.

Luca says:

each fire that is accomplished is a disaster that succumbs.

Luca says:

each Sawn wood is a disaster announced.

Luca says:

If we love someone, we love a forest, even if it's none.

Luca says:

If love the air pure, we go into a forest, that there is certainly.

Luca says:

If we love the forest, God reward us.

Luca says:

If we love life, love it with a forest, what a welcome.

Luca says:

The oxygen that we breathe is free, and you don't seem strange, that the trees, give it as long as they love.

Luca says:

The life that surrounds us, you love, and there is no shadow.

Luca says:

Respect the life of all living beings, and the trees will be pleased.

Luca says:

If you want life to be long, good air, and in the forest, the air it's perfect.

Luca says:

You respect life, whoever it is.

The last cry of the forest

Luca says: Trees such as linden, platinum, horse chestnut, maples, major ash, plant rate, the holly, oak, elms, mulberry, etc. etc. are lacking from our woods. Luca goes out of his way to explain how important the forest is and a very high variety of plants that must stay there, because so there will be a greater variety of animals, insects and birds.

Luca says this because it is understood by those who have the power to put these thoughts into practice.

But how do you fight against a system that exists for years where you put ahead the money first and then the common good in this case of the forest.

There are then a multitude of people who of these my words my feelings do not care nothing, it is much better to pass inside to a forest without understanding the utility that must have the forest, that to get to think that this should be a good haven of insects, animals, birds and plants, to be redone from those in the way of extinction, to those that are in greater numbers, and protect this diversity of living beings.

But think Luca, there are still people who fire the woods what you want to hope that things change.

Luca says: I try to shout it to the four winds in the hope that someone hears, hopefully my thoughts come to the right ear.

Amazon

Di Piantini Antonio

They flew with an airplane over the Amazon rainforest, was the largest merchant of timbers in Brazil, went on patrol to choose the parts of forest from sawing for timber to send in Europe and the United States of America, when at some point the airplane engine goes into smoke he touches to make an emergency landing over the forest trees. The airplane splits into two, and the crew remain alive only in two merchants Antonio and his wife Maria.

Once you get down to the ground, Antonio asks to Maria: Dear is all right, nothing broke.

Maria: No, and you dear

Antonio: No I have not broken

anything, just a few scratches but nothing serious; and now we are doing Maria.

Maria: I do not know, we try to recover from the airplane what can be useful, we look if the radio still works.

Antonio: I watch if the radio still goes or not.

Antonio takes the radio and tries to see if it works, but after several attempts he realizes that it is broken.

Antonio: nothing to do, the radio is broken.

He says to the wife, down here for tonight then tomorrow we will see about to be done, now let's turn on a fire to keep the animals away and if we do we try to sleep.

The meeting

The next morning of mutual agreement they decide to head east from the part where the sun rises, take from the remains of the airplane of the raincoats two blankets a knife big enough and a machete that will serve to make their way into the forest and depart. At the beginning there is a lot of effort to make their way because the vegetation is very dense, but after three four kilometers they find a path beaten, and they think that there are some indigenous people nearby. They walk around the path, looking for this people hoping they are not cannibals, but a civilized people.

They walk for a few hours, then have the feeling as if someone followed them, they stop a little for resting, when behind them appear two indigenous, but not equal to all men, but the skin was colored striped like that of a zebra, but instead of being black and white was colored brown and green, perhaps because it had turned into time to camouflage better in the forest, the hair was black and short and the two indigenous were also quite high, about two feet the eyes were large and green and the character was not threatening but rather made of curiosity in seeing two people different from them.

The first dialogue with the indigenous

Maria asks the two indigenous: do you speak our language, we are lost, fell our airplane that is why we are here, we are the only survivors, you understand.

One of the two natives takes the word and says: Yes, I'm Life and his name is Praise, these are the names that gave us the missionary lived with us for nine years, then he died, but he was always alive in our hearts was just a good man.

What your name, and why are you here?

Maria replies: my name is Maria and he is called Antonio, we are here to study the forest, we are two botanists.

Lying their true purpose of why they were there.

Praise took the word and asked: you want to come with us, we are going to our village you can eat them something.

Antonio says: We come very gladly, we are hungry and we are tired so we will rest.

Praise says: follow us and we go.

They set out on their way to the path and Antonio and Maria admired the beauty of the forest the magnificent plants and birds that there were many, the animals that appeared and then escaped from all parts, also admired the flowers that there were many and all wonderful.

Arrival in the village

They walked in the forest for about two hours before arriving at the village which was composed of huts in circles, and in the middle a much larger hut where they gathered to eat and to talk about hunting and other things.

Antonio and Maria were taken to the great hut and began to make them questions, because they were there and what they wanted to do etc.

Antonio asked if they knew a few streets where cars or trucks were passing by. Life that was what he knew best their tongue replied of yes, and that it was twenty days of walking in the forest and touching across a river that was now in full cause the rainy season and it was not possible to cross it.

Life explained that in about thirty days cease the rains and the waters will be lowered and then you can cross. Antonio and Maria remained a little disappointed, and now that they do, they asked the chieftains if they could stay there with them until you could cross the river. The tribe leaders accepted, but they also said that they had to participate in the living of the tribe, such as hunting, fishing and cooking, so it was decided.

The first time to hunt

The next day they woke up at dawn to go hunting, Praise asked Antonio if he wanted to participate too, Antonio glad to make this new experience replied of yes.

He dressed and in a second was already ready, the hunters were in four Praise, Life and two more older men, armed with bows and peashooters all those with poisoned arrows that caused the death of the animals in a few seconds without making them suffer.

They set out on their way to the forest and as animals were so many, after half an hour they had already taken the meat for two days. Life the chief of all said that for today was enough and they could return to the village, while they were in the forest praise explained to Antonio what It needed that plant, what the tree was for and so the whole way back. Antonio was fascinated by what he was learning about the forest, to understand that every tree or plant served something or to eat or to heal from so many diseases, in short everything was useful to something, Antonio thought of what was the damage that made his own sawmills in the forest to take only a few trees for wood precious destroying all the other trees.

The return to the village

The day was not finished when they returned to the village, the animals killed and the herbs taken in the forest delivered them to the women who immediately put themselves to cook them, the men tired of the journey were resting on the hammocks and waited for lunch time, only Praise, plant expert, he talked to Antonio about the importance of the forest for the life of the tribe, both because it provided food for the whole tribe, and because the plants provided so many natural medicines and the same plants also provided feed for the forest animals that were then hunted by the tribe's men.

Antonio was explaining what plant was needed to make the poison for the arrows, then what tree was needed to remove the headache, because he had it and he wanted to cure it.

Then Praise lifted up and went with Antonio in the forest, arrived at a tree taken of the leaves and returned to the village, then explain to Antonio that once boiled the leaves you could drink the water and after a while he would take off his headache.

Antonio a little incredulous drank the water, and placed himself lying over a hammock to wait for the headache to pass, Maria in a while gave a hand in the kitchen.

The great evening meal

To prepare food we had first of all to peel the animals taken, then make them to large pieces sprinkle them with aromatic herbs after take a small piece of wood of 4 or 5 centimeters split it to meta for the longitudinal sense but not everything to the bottom because the meat prepared before had to enter the wood then tied to the extremity because the meat did not fall to make the tip from the opposite side then stick in the ground the stick with the meat for pillow block next to the fire and wait for the meat to cook from that part for then to turn it and cook it on the opposite side and lunch was ready.

The first to taste that flesh were just Antonio and Maria mmm a delicacy, they ate to satiety the whole tribe because the meat was so much, but that animals were those eaten Antonio and Maria never knew it, because so much was the variety of animals in the forest that only the natives recognized them and gave him a name of its own used only by the tribe.

After this eaten at loud it had been evening in a while it would have been dark so all the inhabitants headed to their own hut, while Antonio and Maria remained sleeping in the large central hut lying above the hammocks.

The breakfast

Morning at dawn they wake up all in the village they gather under the central hut to decide which way to go in the forest to take the fruit that will serve for breakfast.

Gaia the wife of Life, was the one who commanded the group of women and said: let us women to take the fruit and will also come Maria with us if she wants. Maria all happy because she went into the forest said: I will gladly come, I am leaving the village and I learn something more about the forest. They departed so all together from the village and went into the forest.

After a hundred meters they began to find trees and bushes with fruit, Gaia told Maria to take the necessary fruit for breakfast and no more, because the one that remains on the plant will be good for the next morning and so mull nothing.

Picking up the fruit, while they

went back to the village, Maria looked at the wonderful flowers and the beautiful trees, and thought that if that land bought him her husband for the sawmills would have gone all destroyed, and the villagers would be sent away either by force and both because after that there would be nothing left to eat. This thought made him take a knot at the throat difficult to send down.

A day in the village

Upon reaching the village with lots of fruit, they all gathered under the central hut, and ate themselves. The fruit was great, sweet flavorful of a strange but great taste, they all made a great bellyful, and when they had finished eating Praise he said to Antonio if he wanted to go with him in the forest to take a root of a tree that served for the poison of arrows,

Antonio very pleased he said, and armed with machete, they left for the forest.

In the village there was not much to do, the game taken the day before was enough for today, it was to be cooked but they would do it later, so wax the time to devote themselves to make new arrows, to pin the lances that served to fish, while the children played in the square, the women dedicated themselves to cleaning the huts the large square the great central hut and then they put themselves to rest in the hut and to speak among themselves of the more and less, in short to enjoy the beautiful day that was there.

Maria was speaking with Gaia on what to be made after to cook the meat and how great she had been cooked the day ahead, Gaia told her that today they would cook in another way, and assure Maria that would be good even that way.

Maria and Gaia talk about life in the city

Gaia, a little curious asked Maria:

But the world where you and Antonio come from how it is?

Oh did Mary is not easy to explain however I try to say Maria, the world from where we come we are full of many objects, from the airplane like what we came to us, there are cars and trucks to move fast on the ground to bring objects or people from one place to another, there are houses instead of huts as you have here, houses can be up even more than one hundred meters or low a dozen meters and large hundred square meters or even more, and inside the houses there are so many objects such as the TV that is an object where you see images from around the world, there is a room dedicated to the kitchen where there is the refrigerator which is a mobile to keep the cold from eating there is even the gas that would be a fire that will turn on or off to your liking when there is to cook there is the water in the kitchen but also in the bathrooms where you wash.

And then as an object of exchange you use the card not so big called money and with the money you can buy what you want as long as what you want is for sale and you have enough money.

There are big buildings called sheds where people go to work that is to create items to sell and make money and there inside there are all day to earn money to buy food and to buy items that you need or like, in short everything turns in return to the money you can get more you have more live better and then there are taxes to pay, more stuff to and more money you have to pay to the state that would be a place where there are so many people who spend the money of taxes to create hospitals i.e. where people go to cure diseases, then also to create roads where they pass cars or trucks. To keep the cities in order with sewers i.e. where it goes to end the dirty water, and keep clean from the filthy cities.

And then there are laws that if you do not respect them you go to jail that is a small place where you close together with other people and you can no longer go out until it has been established by a judge, that would be a person who enforces the laws and declares the punishment is the days you have to stay in jail or give money for the punishment you deserve.

In short says Maria is a great chaos to live there with all the laws all taxes the hectic work that there is, it's just a big mess, looking at you here that you enjoy the nature day by day without laws without taxes without having to get up in the morning and go to work all day I can't judge who is better if we or you, here you all know each other, in the city you do not even know in the usual palace. But who knows who is better.

Maria still tells Gaia

Curious Gaia tells Maria: tell me something else from the world where you come from?

Maria says: all right I'll tell you other things, for example there is the current that serves to illuminate the streets of the city and there is the light also inside the houses, which in addition to illuminating the current serves to send all the appliances as: the TV the phono that serves to dry the hair after showering, the water heater, which serves to heat the water, the kitchen oven that serves to cook food, and then there are many other appliances, the electric current also serves in factories to send machines that do many kinds of work, also serves in offices to send computers and other machinery.

Then the most hateful thing is that there are also factories that build weapons: like the rifles that serve both to kill animals and to kill men, then they also build other types of weapons such as: the tanks fighting airplanes and many other weapons to kill people both civilians and soldiers.

Maybe says Maria to Gaia many of those things that I said you, you do not even understand because you have never seen but believe me that the world is much better here than there.

The poison for arrows

Meanwhile Praise and Antonio who had gone into the forest they had found the tree which had the poisonous roots, not to waste the plant raised a root and took only that and covered the hole with the earth that they had done to remove the root, so the tree would not have dried up and would be served to another time. Done this work they took the path to return to the village and as they walked Praise as he used to do, he explained to Antonio what the plant needed, to what the other one needed, in short both to cure illnesses and to eat, every plant needed something.

Antonio was fascinated with the knowledge of Praise and listened to him with an open mouth.

Arrived at the village Praise was immediately at work, took the root and with a stone I began to beat it up to make so many tiny pieces then the taken and put it in a bowl of terracotta added some water and put it on the fire to boil after about an hour, in the bowl had remained a black cookie and stinky, that was the poison to kill the animals, now it was enough to immerse the arrows and let it dry until it was dry. The women meanwhile had already put the flesh of the day ahead in a pot of coarse terracotta to boil over the fire with all the herbs to flavor the meat.

After about an hour and half the flesh was ready to be eaten, then the whole tribe gathered under the central hut to eat. The food was great with all those herbs that had flavored the meat was just exquisite.

It was evening and when they had finished eating they all got up and went to the huts to go to sleep.

The Fish fishing in the ditch

The next morning at the dawn they wake up all, the sweet chirping of the birds cheers the awakening and so all the villagers go under the central hut to decide what to do today and what to eat as lunch, by mutual agreement they decided to eat, in the morning the usual breakfast based on fruit and for lunch eat the fish.

So they organized on who has to go fishing and who has to go to collect the fruit, the younger women have to go to collect the fruit with the baskets, while the men have to go fishing with the older children.

Everyone wait under the hut the return of the women with fruit to have breakfast, but while waiting for men prepare the equipment that serves to fish. Meanwhile they wait they speak also in which ditch to go to catch the fish.

After a short time, the women return with baskets full of fruit, so everyone gets to have breakfast, and the variety of fruit is so much and all good, Antonio and Maria tasted a bit of it all up to satiety.

Antonio finished breakfast joins the men who go fishing and leaves with them.

They walked in the forest to the ditch, the men had brought with them the bows and spears while the children fished with their hands under the stones, they took with bows and lances several big fish while the children took smaller fish, filled the baskets of fish they calculated that it would be enough for two days, so they stopped fishing and as they were in the ditch and wax so much water they all together also a nice bathroom.

Finished the fun of bathing they went on their way to the village and when they were inside the forest, Praise found good mushrooms to eat, took even those and after a short walk arrived at the village.

The women came to meet him and when they saw the mushrooms and all those fish immediately took the baskets and went to prepare to eat. The fish roasted on the fire and the fried mushrooms were a delicious lunch, all young and old ate it to satiety, finished eating since it was getting dark, everyone went to their hut to go to sleep.

In search of mushrooms

Upon waking up as every morning the women including Maria go into the forest looking for fruit to have breakfast, while the men gather in the big hut to decide what to do today. Praise in the meeting intervenes and says: since the good mushrooms are born because we do not go looking for those today, so even if we find many you can dry and eat even later. The men talk about it among themselves and decide to do as has said Praise, so made breakfast with the fruit all are prepared to go to look for mushrooms, take the baskets and away to seek mushrooms in the forest. Praise from true expert teaches everyone to recognize which they are the good mushrooms from the bad ones and poisonous if eaten.

The children each mushroom found, ran from Praise to be told whether the fungus found is good or no, and Praise with so much patience taught them how to recognize the good mushrooms from the poisonous ones.

And so we go on looking for mushrooms until the baskets were all full, the fun was so much then at the return they began to calculate who had found the largest mushroom and who had found the most beautiful to see each other, in short it was a wonderful day and Antonio and Maria had never had much fun so.

When they arrived at the village, the women immediately cleaned the mushrooms to cook them and to eat together with the fish of yesterday. The men put on fire, and the women cooked the fish and in a pot they cooked the mushrooms.

While waiting for lunch to be ready, the men set out to rest on the hammocks and talk about the more and less.

When the meal was ready to eat, everyone took the bowl to put in meal and they passed in front of the women who filled the bowls with mushrooms and in a leaf they put on the fish roasted on the fire. The food was great so much so that Antonio took another bit, then sated he put himself to rest and wait dark on the hammock. After about an hour I begin to get darkness so everyone went into their huts to sleep.

Antonio and Maria decided to live with the tribe

The days passed in extreme tranquility in comparison of the city that came Antonio and Maria, and stay there with the whole tribe was very beautiful and as Antonio and Maria had no children and being there with all those children in the village they filled the heart with joy.

And then every day there was always to learn something or on the plants of the forest or on the animals or on the insects, or on the fruit, or on the fish or the mushrooms, in short every day they learned something and had understood how important the forest for all the tribes that lived there.

Past thirty days the rains had diminished and perhaps the river was no longer full but before leaving they decided to wait another week.

In the week that had to pass before leaving Antonio and Maria spoke among themselves of what would have been nice to live there with the tribe of Life and Praise, so they took courage and asked the tribal leaders if they could, once been in the city, return to live with them because they loved that kind of living life until death. The tribal leaders reasoned among themselves and made a decision, they could live with them, Antonio and Maria were pleased for the decision taken by the tribal leaders.

Return to the city

After seven days came the day they had to leave, reluctantly prepared for the journey that had to last about twenty days, they took food supplies for the trip, greeted everyone with the promise of returning to the village as soon as they would settle all their business in the city, and as a guide for the journey they went along with their life and praise. They left for a few kilometers the path was beaten then began to make their way into the thick of the forest, the fatigue was so much and to find the way they took turns.

When darkness came they lit a fire, because the animals were away from them for fear of fire, they lay in circles around the fire and slept tired of the fatigue of the day.

After twelve days they arrived at the river which was no longer in full, to traverse they took a stick for one and then a pole quite long where one behind the other they kept themselves at this post, so slowly without falling they crossed the river.

After another five days of walking they came to the road where they passed trucks and cars, Antonio said to Life and Praise that he would come back there in that precise place between twenty days but this time they had to come in more people at least ten or more, because he would bring from the city of things useful to the tribe, so they greeted, Life and Praise took the path just made to return to the village and Antonio and Maria began to wait for some means of transport, after about an hour and half a truck passed that made them go up and bring them into town.

Arrived at home Antonio and Maria put immediately for sale the house then Antonio went to the sawmills and gave the order to workers to dismantle all installations for sawing and to give them to those who picks up the old iron. Antonio did so because his sawmills could no longer saw any tree in the forest, this also sold the land where there were sawmills.

With the money proceeded with the sale of all that he had, he went where they sell the land of the forest and buy all and even a little more, the forest where there was the tribe of Life and he headed the land of the forest right to the tribe so that no one could saw those sunrises so important for the life of the tribe.

With the little money left Antonio and Maria bought things that would serve the tribe, such as pots, frying pans, matches to turn on the fire, etc. etc.

And for the little ones they bought five rubber balloons, balls for play bowls, skittles, two skipping ropes, etc.

Waited for the one hundred and twenty days Antonio and Maria departed from the city with all the stuff bought to go to the appointment that had given Life and Antonio. Arrived Life and the ten men were there to wait, Antonio descended from the truck and as first he gave the contract of the land to Life, and explain to him the importance of that sheet of paper he had and told him never to lose it because that paper established that the land was master the tribe did this unload the stuff bought from the truck if they put it off and all together they left for the village.

The trip was very tiring for the so much stuff to wear, but slowly they arrived at the village, the children remained open-mouthed for all the toys they had brought, and they were so pleased also Antonio and Maria for having changed their lives, without having to rush behind the money to pay taxes to pay to eat, be without laws become free.

Free to enjoy the long or short life it is.

Opinions dedicated to me

By Giulia

I read your book and I have to tell you that it was a very nice gift for me.

I lived with your thoughts distant memories still alive in my mind.

My childhood I lived here in these valleys and like you I loved and love all the nature and the beautiful redwoods.

Yours are not thoughts of a mentally ill...... the sick are we who cannot go any further...... we cannot see and feel what life gives us.

Your words will open your heart and mind who will be ready......

Others remain in their inner silence.

Giulia

By Francesco

Dear Antonio,

Yours is a beautiful book where you express your great love for plants, animals and nature.

It is also a great act of love for your wife and girls.

The important thing is the criticism of the system created by the man who is destroying the most beautiful exists in the creation not understanding that the common good is more important than our individual selfishness.

Just one note I'll make you for the title (turn it into Antonio's thoughts).

Francesco B.

By Gisella

There is a lot of serenity, self-irony and love for the things that surround you.

Beautiful is when you talk about your wife Maria, the daughters of the stimulus that have given you even in the "blind" moments of your life; Infinite richness as the sequoias secular plants present as "sandstone" in the book, as a symbol of the static, the strength and the richness!

Good Antonio, keep writing, there is "so much" there inside, someone definitely reading it will inner wealth and strength to fight, always!!

By Dr. Luigi

Antonio has experienced the restlessness of a troubled existence, but never desperate.

He has the pure heart of a boy.

His writing excites for the strong desire to communicate a part of his life characterized by the naïve certainties of simple people.

His redwoods send silent messages to heaven, his characters struggle for the conquest of a denied serenity.

With the wishes of a future as clear as possible from breathlessness.

Dr. Luigi

I cordially thank all the people who have given me a bit of their precious time to write my own opinions about my book.

Antonio Piantini

www.ingramcontent.com/pod-product-compliance
Lightning Source LLC
Chambersburg PA
CBHW060509290526
45791CB00001B/332